KIN

BY BATHSHEBA DORAN

DRAMATISTS
PLAY SERVICE
INC.

For Katie

ACKNOWLEDGMENTS

I am indebted to a great number of people for the development of this play, not least the original cast. To their names I must aadd Dominic D'Andrea, Jennifer Van Dyck, Jenny Maguire, Jenny Worton, Jordan Harrison, Jonathan Walker, Kathryn Grody, Katie Doran, Knud Adams, Lucy Smith, Mark Subias, Megan Monahgan Rivas, Paul Steinberg, Peter MacRobbie and Polly Lee. Thank you to everyone that is the Lark Play Development Center, South Coast Repertory Theater and Playwrights Horizons, particularly Adam Greenfield and Tim Sanford for extraordinary dramaturgical wisdom. Above all thank you to Sam Gold for all the suggestions, insistences and insight.

KIN was presented by Playwrights Horizons (Tim Sanford, Artistic Director; Leslie Marcus, Managing Director; Carol Fishman, General Manager) in New York City, opening on March 21, 2011. It was directed by Sam Gold; the set design was by Paul Steinberg; the costume design was by David Zinn; the lighting design was by Jane Cox; the sound design was by Matt Tierney; the dialect coach was Stephen Gabis; the production manager was Christopher Boll; and the production stage manager was Alaina Taylor. The cast was as follows:

LINDA	Suzanne Bertish
MAX	Bill Buell
ANNA	Kristen Bush
SEAN	Patch Darragh
KAY	Kit Flanagan
HELENA	Laura Heisler
SIMON / GIDEON	Matthew Rauch
ADAM	Cotter Smith
RACHEL	Molly Ward

A NOTE ON DESIGN

When I began writing I thought of this play as taking place in what I found myself referring to as "the landscape of the mind." Many of my characters were based in what I only thought of as "the city." It could have been any major Western Capital — New York, Paris, London, or an imaginary city entirely. Other characters were simply placed "far away." I was attempting to conjure the globe. Eventually I found it helped the story to be specific so now there is a literal geography, but I hope that the director and design team will help recapture my early sense that this play was taking place above all in a non-literal landscape.

A NOTE ON STAGING

This is a play made from largely two-person scenes that is nonetheless about an ensemble. To underline this, my original idea was to have the entire cast onstage for every scene except the first and last. Sam Gold refined this suggestion into something more delicate, complex and idiosyncratic. I now think it suffices to say that I hope future directors will find their own way to maintain a sense of ensemble so that we feel all characters throughout, hidden sometimes, in shadows maybe, but present.

CHARACTERS

ANNA (30s)

ADAM, ANNA'S FATHER (60s)

HELENA (30s)

SEAN (30s)

LINDA, SEAN'S MOTHER (55 – 65)

MAX, LINDA'S BROTHER (55 – 65)

RACHEL (30s)

KAY (60s)

GIDEON (34)

SIMON (40s)

(Gideon and Simon should be played by the same actor. This should not be emphasized, but an unrecognizable transformation is not required.)

TIME AND PLACE

The action of the play takes place over the last seven years in various locations in America and Ireland.

"What can I say? God help me, what can I say? Silence will stifle me ..."

—*Sophocles*, Electra

"I saw a crow running about with a stork. I marveled long and investigated their case in order that I might find the clue as to what it was that they had in common. When amazed and bewildered I approached them then indeed I saw that both of them were lame."

—*Rumi*, Spiritual Couplets

"A man who calls his kinsmen to a feast does not do so to save them from starving. They all have food in their own homes. When we gather together in the moonlit village ground it is not because of the moon. Every man can see it in his own compound. We come together because it is good for kinsmen to do so."

—*Chinua Achebe*, Things Fall Apart

KIN

Scene 1

An office at Columbia University

Anna sits. Simon stands. Everything awkward, uncomfortable.

SIMON. I thought it was best not to leave you dangling, you know? But at this stage of life ... I mean ... I know what I'm looking for, you know what you're looking for, we know what we're looking for, or maybe we don't, maybe that's the thing, maybe I don't know what I'm looking for, but I know it's not you. That sounds terrible, doesn't it? But no, fuck it, I'm trying to be truthful here, let's have truth in human relations for once, how about that? Let's be truthful with one another. I mean, did you think this was going anywhere? Really? *(Anna shakes her head.)* Thank you. Thank you. Now I feel less like an ass. And I mean — I'm so much older than you, that's probably why you picked me, right? A father figure? You lost your dad when you were very young, right? So that was probably part of the attraction, don't you think? But that's not healthy, that's not sustainable, or maybe it is, I don't know.

ANNA. My father's still alive.

SIMON. Oh. Then I'm confusing you with someone else. Sorry. Of course he is. The point is — and this is where I'm the real asshole — I don't know what I want. Not really. I mean, sometimes I think I want something long term, but I've *been* married, you know? And it was no fun. Now maybe that was her, maybe that was me, maybe it was the combination but ... but ... I just want someone I can talk to, you know? And fuck. And we *had* that. I'm not denying it. We had that. But now ... it's over, isn't it? I mean the conversation is over. Can't you just feel it? There's something

11

dead here. The light's gone out. And if the light's gone out, then put out the light. Or maybe not. I don't know ... we could try to ignite it. But love shouldn't be so much effort. Or maybe it should. It's such a fucking construct, you know? Literature is such a fucking *trap*. Unrealistic expectations. I don't know. I'm just so fucking lonely. And I know you are too, maybe that's what brought us together, right? Loneliness. A love of Keats. Your mind, you have a fucking brilliant mind, you know that? Your thesis is fucking brilliant. You're going to have an incredible career, and you'll forget all about me! I'll just be some old professor of yours that you inveigled into bed with your skinny arms and your brilliant mind. Because let's be real. We admire each other, but ... this is even a little sordid. The rest of the faculty knows, I think. Clancy made a veiled comment ... and it's not against the rules, exactly, you are an adjunct and this *is* the English department, we are all poets here, and poets fuck, but Clancy's comment ... I think fundamentally ... it made me feel cheap. And it made you ... cheap by association ... So I think ... You haven't said anything ... Are you going to make this hard on me? Don't. Please don't. This is just human relationships. I wrote a poem once. When I was in my thirties and I still wrote poetry. And I compared a woman's vagina to a revolving door. People come in. They go out. That's life. And you know what my simile for the penis was? A staple gun. In an office. Punch, punch, punch. Revolve, revolve, revolve. That is life. That is the fucking monotony of searching for your soul mate. Okay? I still stand by that. So just ... Did we even love each other?

ANNA. No. *(Simon stares at Anna, hoping for a better cue to exit. He doesn't get one. So he sighs and leaves.)*

Scene 2

Central Park

Midnight.

Helena on the grass, cradling a dead dog. Paroxysms of grief.

HELENA. Zoë! Don't be dead, don't be dead, don't be dead. I love you, I will always love you. Oh my dog! My life partner! My love! How could you die? How could you die and leave me here! I don't even know what to do with your body! They say it's illegal to bury you in the park! You loved the park! They say, they say if I don't have any money I should put you in a bag, in a big black bag, and I should write on the bag "dead dog" and leave you out with the garbage as if you weren't a *soul!* As if you weren't *my* soul! *(Her cell phone rings. Into the phone:)* Anna? Where are you? Where the fuck are you? I need you, Anna, I need you to get here. I'm freaking out, I'm too upset, I can't even see. Tears are literally blinding me. Plus it's dark. Totally. You're right. I'm overreacting. Well, you kind of sound like you think I'm overreacting. *(And now we see Anna on her cell phone. Helena does not see her. Anna does not see Helena. Anna has a flashlight. She turns and the beam from her flashlight hits the sorry sight of Helena and her dead dog.)* There you are.
ANNA. Here I am.
HELENA. *(Eternally grateful.)* You brought a flashlight. So practical.
ANNA. Can I see Zoë? *(She looks at the dog.)* She looks peaceful.
HELENA. You think?
ANNA. Absolutely.
HELENA. I brought a ... *(Helena produces an inadequate gardening tool.)*
ANNA. Do you want me to dig?
HELENA. I'll dig the grave. She was my dog.
ANNA. Of course.

HELENA. Keep watch. Fucking city regulations, I mean what the fuck, it's sick, it's Greek, it's ... what happened to universal space? Isn't it my fucking planet? Wasn't it Zoë's fucking earth? I mean, why does everybody seem to own a piece of the universe but me. Well fuck that, my earth, my dirt, my tax dollars. *(Helena digs. Eventually ...)*

ANNA. The last open grave I saw was my mom's.

HELENA. You know what I'm feeling ... because your mom ... I mean it's probably not the same. Your mom. My dog. That's really offensive. *(Beat.)*

ANNA. I know what you're feeling.

HELENA. I can't imagine what you felt ... I mean ... your mom. And you were just a kid ... and your dad crying, didn't you say you'd never seen him cry before?

ANNA. Never before, never since. I just kept looking at him at the graveside, this strong man, you know, this strong, army man, the Colonel, displays of emotion antithetical to his being. And he was broken, completely broken. My dad was so crippled with grief at the graveside and all I could think was that the way he was crying made me want to fall in love.

Scene 3

Sean's apartment, NYC

Sean on the telephone to his mother, Linda. If we see Linda, she's far, far away and we should feel this.

LINDA. Describe the sky for me, Seany.

SEAN. The sky's black, Mum.

LINDA. Just black?

SEAN. A little grey, a little green even.

LINDA. Any clouds?

SEAN. It's too late at night for clouds.

LINDA. Is it? I get confused. Did I wake you up?

SEAN. No.

LINDA. Silly isn't it. After all these years I can't remember what time it is there, what time it is here. It's yesterday there, isn't it? My yesterday.

SEAN. That's right. It's Saturday. Saturday night.

LINDA. It's Sunday here. Worst day of the week, Sunday. They just drag on and on and —

SEAN. I've been thinking ...

LINDA. *(A joke.)* Don't do that, you'll hurt your head.

SEAN. You could start going to church again. The priest you saw, he's dead now. *(Beat.)* Mum? Claire told me. Two of us were thinking —

LINDA. You and your sister deciding what's best for me. Bit early for that, don't you think? Senility hasn't hit yet. I don't piss and shit myself —

SEAN. Mum.

LINDA. Yet.

SEAN. There's a new priest now. You might like him. Or Claire could take you. *(Beat.)* Mum? *(Beat.)* Don't go quiet, Mum ...

LINDA. Banished, Seany. I was banished.

SEAN. No ...

LINDA. Yes, if you don't repent, you're banished. So I'm banished. That's that. Linda's not welcome in the house of God and Linda doesn't care because I know what I saw through the mist. God isn't good, Seany.

SEAN. The church is changing. It's in the papers all the time. The whole world is. Remember I told you about that woman I'm training? The fat, fat woman? Not fat anymore. Lost eighty-five pounds. She cried! She didn't think it was possible. But change she did. We all have the potential for change.

LINDA. Says who? Where are you getting this stuff?

SEAN. I'm reading a book about it.

LINDA. What kind of book?

SEAN. It's about happiness.

LINDA. *(Sarcastic.)* You'll have to send me a copy.

SEAN. I will. It's a self-help book.

LINDA. A *what*? You've been living in America too long ... You certainly are undergoing a process of change if you're reading a self-help book. *(Beat — then slightly anxious.)* What are you reading that for? *(Beat.)* Seany? *(Beat.)* Don't *you* go quiet ... What are you reading a book about happiness for? Are you sad? Seany?

SEAN. I'm worried about you. Claire says you don't leave the house at all now.

LINDA. Let's not have a conversation with Claire in it, let's have a conversation that's just you and me, all by ourselves.

SEAN. Mum, you can't stay locked up in that house for the rest of your life!

LINDA. *(Beat.)* At night sometimes ... I go to the window, and I open it a tiny little crack, and I listen.

SEAN. What do you hear?

LINDA. *Little* life. Insects and things. I think I'm a night creature. You were always a night creature. You used to be out on Saturday nights.

SEAN. *(Closing off, shutting down.)* I work on Saturdays now. I'm tired.

LINDA. What's the point of living in the big city if you don't go out on the town, Sean? That's what New York's *for*. Painting red. *(Beat.)* Are you lonely, Sean? *(Beat.)* I can hear you being lonely down the telephone. *(Beat.)* Is it that girl?

SEAN. *(Surprised.)* What girl?

LINDA. Rachel. You brought her home for a Christmas. She was Saturday nights. You'd come back sometimes and call me up, drunk and so happy, you were so full of love. You'd say, "I love you, Mum. I love you so much ..." and I could hear her laughing in the background and you sounded so happy, Sean.

SEAN. You know we broke up.

LINDA. Did she hurt you? Did she break your heart?

SEAN. I broke hers.

LINDA. *(Reassured.)* Oh, well then ... Looking for someone else, then, are you?

SEAN. Sure.

LINDA. What kind of person are you looking for?

SEAN. Someone who doesn't freebase.

LINDA. What?

SEAN. Nothing.

LINDA. You're not looking very hard if you're staying indoors on a Saturday night. *(Pause.)*

SEAN. I'm just taking a break, Mum. I'll get back out there.

LINDA. *(Emphatically.)* You should do. You're too good to waste. *(Beat.)*

SEAN. I have to put on my pajamas and go to bed. I have to be back at the gym at six-thirty.

LINDA. If we stay on the phone just a little longer, we'll be talking on the same day of the week. Shall we do that, Seany? Shall I describe the sky to you? Imagine a bucket of off-white paint. Do you see it?

SEAN. I do.

LINDA. Now stir in some black paint. Just a little bit. Stir it and stir it and stir it and stir it until it's nearly mixed through but not quite … that's what the sky looks like. Like dirty seagulls or dirty doves.

SEAN. I see it.

LINDA. I see yours. Black, green, like witches.

SEAN. Had a few drinks, have you?

LINDA. *(Distant.)* Oh, who cares what I do with my time? It passes.

Scene 4

Columbia University campus

Anna and Helena on a bench. Sandwiches. Spring. Helena crying.

ANNA. I'm so sorry.

HELENA. That's what she said to me. "Maybe it's time for you to get another dog." In this like … bored tone. Like my grief is boring to her. Maybe it is. Maybe it's boring to you.

ANNA. It's not —

HELENA. It's boring to me actually. Feelings are boring. but they're *life*, what can you do? And my mother, my fucking mother, she thinks I should just buy another dog and magically … And I get it. I mean, it's been a year. It's just that she was all I had.

ANNA. That's not true.

HELENA. She's who I slept with every night. I mean she knew everything about me. Everything. She knew when I ate, when I cried, when I took a crap. And I loved her. It doesn't stop being real love just because it's a *dog*. I mean, if it had been another human being that I had lived with for fifteen years that suddenly died, if I had walked home and found a human being dead on the floor, lying in their own shit and piss with a look of pain, of twisted pain on their face, then a year later nobody would be surprised if I was still *upset*. Or would they? Who the fuck knows? People want other people to be perky.

ANNA. Look. Grief is hard. That's what love does to us. It hurts us, right?

HELENA. I don't think it's supposed to. Not always.

ANNA. Because of death, though. Love always hurts the one that's left behind.

HELENA. Right.

ANNA. You're supposed to grieve for something you loved. *(Helena hugs Anna.)*

HELENA. Thank you for meeting me on your lunch break in the freezing cold! *(Anna gets a thick manuscript out of her bag.)* You'll think this is crazy but sometimes I can still feel Zoë with me ...

ANNA. *(Ignoring that, passing the manuscript.)* You're the first person I've given this to.

HELENA. Is this...?

ANNA. I want to hear everything you have to say about it.

HELENA. "Keats' Punctuation."

ANNA. I need to find a snappier title. Any section you don't understand, I want to know about. Because I want it to be accessible, you know? And not just read by other Keats scholars. I tried to make it ... at least ... the middle is kind of boring —

HELENA. Don't say that!

ANNA. But the beginning and the end ... I tried to get to some place ... human.

HELENA. You're so frickin' incredible, you know that? I am so proud of you. You finished!

ANNA. It's just a first draft —

HELENA. It is a big deal. It is a big frickin' deal. *(They hug.)*

ANNA. I have to go teach. Don't you have to get back to work?

HELENA. No.

ANNA. How come?

HELENA. Because at five P.M. today, little ol' Helena has a little ol' audition.

ANNA. Oh, that's great!

HELENA. Would you like to guess for what play?

ANNA. No.

HELENA. *A Midsummer Night's Dream.* Would you like to guess for what part?

ANNA. I just don't have time.

HELENA. Helena! Isn't that crazy? Don't you think that *means* something? That *her* name is already *my* name? I already know what it's like to answer as Helena, I mean I know that's superficial but ... I don't know. It feels meaningful to me right now. And she's such a strong woman, you know? That's how I see her. Strong. Guess where the production is?

ANNA. Where?

HELENA. Here! Columbia! A student production! Which is great because that means it will really be about the work and it just never is when you're trying to sell tickets, but they don't sell tickets for student productions so ...

ANNA. Is it paid? *(Helena sighs. The sigh becomes a stony silence.)* I was just asking because if it's a graduate thesis production they do pay the actors so —

HELENA. I don't know if it's paid.

ANNA. If it's not, you can claim back on your tax return. Call it an in-kind donation.

HELENA. Whatever. Maybe it's paid. Maybe it's not. I'd just like to be working again. Not everything is about taxes, Anna. I don't even do my taxes.

ANNA. Oh.

HELENA. I could hang around after my audition and we could get a drink around here. I frickin' miss student bars.

ANNA. I can't. I have a date.

HELENA. *(Disappointed.)* Who is it this time?

ANNA. A critic.

HELENA. *(Horrified.)* No ...

ANNA. The machine kept matching me with lawyers and bankers. I adjusted my search criteria last week. Now it's matching me with journalists.

HELENA. You know, Anna, the hunt for the soul mate, that is a mysterious thing, and I don't care how much you pay this website, the big old American dollar is not going to short-cut that process. What if you're supposed to be with a coal miner or something? Or an acrobat? But the machine can't think out of the box, the machine keeps hooking you up with Ivy League a-holes.

ANNA. It's my fault. Those are the guys I'm getting because those are the things I said were important to me. Education. Ambition. Money.

HELENA. You said money?

ANNA. Well ... sure ...

HELENA. *(Pure judgment.)* Wow.

ANNA. If this one's a disaster, I'll change my search criteria.

HELENA. The very fact that there are criteria is a problem.

ANNA. An acrobat?

HELENA. I find it really offensive that you would go on a date with a critic. It's the equivalent of dating someone who's trying to kill me. *(Beat.)* Want to hear my audition speech?

ANNA. I have to go. Break a leg. *(Anna exits.)*

HELENA. Hey Anna!

    I am as ugly as a bear,

    For beasts that meet me run away for fear ...

Scene 5

Linda's house, Ireland

Late at night. Linda and Max sit, drinks in hand, staring out into space.

LINDA. Sean's out tonight. Out on a date.

MAX. That's nice.

LINDA. A girl he met. On the internet.

MAX. On the internet?

LINDA. Not in a dirty way, in an organized way when they give details about the kind of person that they want to meet and —

MAX. I gotcha. Millie's cousin Marion was married that way.

LINDA. Really?

MAX. She was, she met a man through an internet website —

LINDA. That's it. It's a website —

MAX. Enthusiasts of cheese, I think it was —

LINDA. No, this is different —

MAX. And they got along and within six months he'd popped the question. Now she's pregnant and they're talking about moving to Greece to set up a B and B.

LINDA. All Sean does now is go on dates.

MAX. Very nice.

LINDA. Tonight he dates a facialist.

MAX. What the fuck is a facialist?

LINDA. They squeeze your face and make it pretty.

MAX. *What?*

LINDA. That's what they do.

MAX. Why would squeezing your face make it pretty? It would make it blotchy I should think.

LINDA. Faces are full of pus.

MAX. Mine isn't.

LINDA. Everyone's is.

MAX. Mine isn't.

LINDA. Every time I talk to him he's going on a date. "Can't talk, Mum. Going on a date." "Getting ready for a date." "Out on a date." He is *obsessed* with the word date. I told him, "Only the people in the pictures go on dates." He took it the wrong way.

MAX. Kids *always* take things the wrong fucking way. You can't open your fucking mouth without them pointing out that you just *fucked* something for them. Like my girl, Janie. She's got emotional problems.

LINDA. Since when?

MAX. Since her *therapist* said so. And I swear to God, every single time I open my fucking mouth she says I'm belittling her. Every time I use the word "fucking," *she* says *he* says it's aggressive. So now I have to try and not use the word around her. And you know *why* she's got emotional problems? Do you know why every single kid in her generation has emotional problems?

LINDA. They're weak.

MAX. Their expectations are too fucking high! Animals are fucking happy. Not people.

LINDA. I kept Claire and Sean's expectations *very* low. They're happier as adults than they were as children, the only person they have to thank for that is me. There's nothing about it in the books, but there's something to be said for providing an upward trajectory.

MAX. Since Janie's been in counseling, the only topic of conversation on offer is, "Remember when you broke my heart by not taking me fucking ice skating after you promised."

LINDA. Mine still criticize. Well, not Seany so much, course he's not here to criticize, but Claire … "Remember the time," she'll say, "after Dad left and you didn't get out of bed for three days and I had to make the sandwiches?" *(Beat.)* What does she fucking want me to do about it *now?*

MAX. Stop saying "fucking!" You're emotionally damaging me!

LINDA. Claire's not making too good a parent herself. She dropped the baby the other day.

MAX. Whoops! *(They roar with laughter. Pause.)* Shouldn't criticize them. Not really.

LINDA. Why not? They sit around and complain about us.

MAX. I'm not saying I couldn't have done better. I'm not saying that. *(Beat.)* No, I am saying that. I will say that. I didn't drink much, worked hard, helped with homework, I mean what do they want? Jesus Christ could have fathered my Janie and she'd have said, "Remember that time you were supposed to take me ice skating, but you had to go deal with the loaves and the fishes?" *(Beat.)* And the reason I didn't take her ice skating was that I had band practice! Had to give it up in the end though, didn't I? And I don't call her up and say "Remember when I gave up my rock band because there weren't enough hours in the day with everybody needing something from me!" *(Beat.)* It's nice to be drunk. I haven't been drunk in a long time.

LINDA. Millie keeps you on a tight leash —

MAX. She made me promise I wouldn't get stinking. And I am stinking.

LINDA. What does she expect? You and I always got drunk together. Since we were kiddies.

MAX. You've drunk enough booze tonight to sink a bloody battleship.

LINDA. Bollocks. I can drink, and drink, and drink, and drink and it doesn't do a thing to me.

MAX. It's doing something to you, Linda. *(Beat.)* What time is it? I should call Millie. *(He stands.)*

LINDA. Can't I have you to myself for one fucking night?

MAX. I was just going to go in the other room for a *second* …

LINDA. Does Millie understand that you and I never see each other since she moved you to the other side of Ireland?

MAX. Linda, it will just take a minute.

LINDA. Oh, a minute now, is it? First it was a second, then a minute, then you'll be gone for a full half-hour, talking to one another. *(Worked up.)* I see you once in a fucking blue moon and I can't have you all

22

to myself for one night?

MAX. Ah, you're behaving badly now, that's the alcohol, that's what it's doing to you … *(Beat. He thinks of a solution.)* I'll text her. *(He gets out his phone. He inexpertly texts his wife.)* It's probably better anyway. She'll only be cross at me for drinking.

LINDA. *(Fixing him with a stare.)* What are you telling her?

MAX. I'm writing that I love her. *(Linda rolls her eyes, but says nothing.)*

LINDA. Does Millie know? That tonight's the anniversary?

MAX. Of course.

LINDA. The anniversary of my death.

MAX. Don't say that.

LINDA. My ending, the termination of little Linda was twenty-one years ago tonight. And back then she was pretty as a picture. Remember her? A young thing in a yellow dress. And then boom! As old as the cliffs. *(Beat.)* And where's he tonight, I wonder?

MAX. Who?

LINDA. The man in the mist. At home with his family? Playing with his children? *(Max claps his hands.)*

MAX. Don't get maudlin.

LINDA. Get what?

MAX. Maudlin.

LINDA. I don't even know what that means.

MAX. Mournful. Morbid. Melancholy.

LINDA. How'd you ever hear a word like that?

MAX. It's just a word.

LINDA. Think I'm stupid now, do you?

MAX. No.

LINDA. Maudlin. I'm entitled to be maudlin, I think. Tonight. Do you mind if I'm maudlin for one fucking night? I never *tell* anyone how I feel! I never talk about the nightmares! I never repeat what plays round and around in my head. It's a lot of fucking energy to stay silent, Max! Can I indulge myself a little tonight? On the fucking anniversary! *(Beat.)*

MAX. Say whatever you want, Linda.

LINDA. I want to die … I want to be dead …

MAX. Always?

LINDA. I don't know.

MAX. I know I made fun of the counseling before but … for you it's different. It's deserved … I could pay if you'd like to see a person who is trained in ... your pain, Linda.

LINDA. I don't think ... I don't think ... I can do it. I had the counseling at the time and it didn't ... *(Distress, panic.)* I'm too sad. Everybody says. It's why Martin left. He'd come home, I'd be staring into space. "I'm so sorry, Martin," I'd say. "I'll get myself together." "Don't worry," he'd say. "You're entitled." But I never let him touch me again, and then he was gone.

MAX. Martin was a bastard.

LINDA. Cost me my husband, that man in the mist. And then my son.

MAX. No ...

LINDA. He's why Sean left! Now he's out on a date! He'll marry out there and never come back!

MAX. He's a young man, Linda! That's what young men do! They go out in the world! They seek adventure!

LINDA. All the tiny little stones I picked from his tiny little cuts on his tiny little knees and he's gone. Bought a pair of long trousers and off he went across the sea, not a look over his shoulder, not a word of apology. You spend every last pence you have on them! The constant buying of things for children! The T-shirts and posters and key rings, pound after pound after pound and then boom! Grown men and women and you're at their mercy! I wish I hadn't come back! I wish I had jumped! The man in the mist had killed me so what was the fucking point!

MAX. Linda, you wanted to live. You want to live ...

LINDA. *(In pieces.)* I'm sorry, Max! I know this must be awful for you!

MAX. *(Grim.)* You're my sister. It's the least I can fucking do.

Scene 6

Kay's house, D.C.

Kay wears pajamas.

KAY. What the hell are you doing here, Colonel? You're supposed to be in New York.
ADAM. Surprise?
KAY. You're supposed to be spending the night at Anna's.
ADAM. Surprise.
KAY. You said you weren't coming to D.C. until tomorrow.
ADAM. It is tomorrow.
KAY. It's 4 A.M.!
ADAM. I'm just a little early.
KAY. Something's wrong. I swear to God, I don't see you from one year to the next, then you show up like a bad penny and spill your guts.
ADAM. I thought it would be like the old days in Texas. Me knocking on your door in the middle of the night, hoping for ...
KAY. *(Playful.)* Hoping for what?
ADAM. Hoping to see you.
KAY. Give me a kiss. *(Adam looks around him. The room is mostly bare.)*
ADAM. What happened here?
KAY. Everything's in storage. I told you on the phone. I'm taking a trip.
ADAM. For how long?
KAY. A while.
ADAM. You're renting the place out?
KAY. Selling.
ADAM. Where do you plan on living when you get home?
KAY. I haven't made any definite plans.
ADAM. Why haven't you made any definite plans?
KAY. Because it's liberating.
ADAM. Just how sick are you? *(Pause. Adam continues to study the empty space.)*

KAY. You were going to have a drink in your hand when I told you. *(Beat.)* I have defeated Western medicine. So I'm headed east. To India. I shall see mystical people. Maybe they'll wave their hands over me and make it all go away. *(Adam starts to ask another question.)* And then I was going to tell you that I don't want to talk about it anymore. It's not my favorite subject. *(Beat. Adam nods.)*

ADAM. I shouldn't have woken you up.

KAY. But you did, so why don't you tell me what's wrong? Why didn't you stay at Anna's?

ADAM. It's not important anymore.

KAY. Of course it is.

ADAM. Forget it. *(Beat.)*

KAY. So how is Anna?

ADAM. Good.

KAY. Last time I saw you she was at Columbia, right?

ADAM. She's teaching there now. Got her Ph.D.

KAY. *Doctor* Anna.

ADAM. She's writing a book.

KAY. What's it about?

ADAM. Nothing. Punctuation. She's been telling me about the damn thing for years, I have no idea what she's talking about.

KAY. Punctuation's important.

ADAM. Is it?

KAY. Sure. Without it nothing would make any sense. Period.

ADAM. Our conversations are a blast. She tells me about her work which I don't understand, and I can't tell her about my work because it's classified.

KAY. *(Beat.)* Is she seeing anyone? *(Adam sighs.)* Aha. Who?

ADAM. A personal trainer. What kind of job *is* that?

KAY. Fitness and such. The two of you probably have a lot in common.

ADAM. I am a colonel in the United States Armed Forces, Kay. I am not a fitness instructor.

KAY. *(Amused.)* Sorry.

ADAM. She brought him to dinner! No warning, just brought him to dinner. I mean, maybe I wouldn't have minded so much if this guy had anything to recommend him, you know. He didn't even tuck his shirt in. He's Irish.

KAY. Sexy.

ADAM. I'm not one of those Americans who's sappy about

Ireland. *(Beat.)* I asked if he planned to go back, he didn't even answer. He just shrugged. Language is not his first language, if you know what I mean.

KAY. Maybe he was shy.

ADAM. His father's dead. His mother ... I could not get a clear picture of the mother. I did gather that she was unemployed.

KAY. Adam. Honey. You're not supposed to like him. He's screwing your daughter. *(Beat.)* Has she ever brought any other boy to dinner?

ADAM. No.

KAY. So this one's important.

ADAM. They were clamped together at this restaurant. Physically clamped. Finally, he goes to the bathroom and she says, "For the first time I really understand what you and Mom had."

KAY. Oh boy.

ADAM. And she's glowing, you know? Just glowing. I felt sick.

KAY. Adam ...

ADAM. We're strangers! She put her hand on my arm, looked into my eyes, and she was a stranger. And then the personal trainer came back from the bathroom, sat down, stuck his arm around her like she was his property, and I picked up the check.

KAY. Adam ...

ADAM. I could hear my dead wife laughing.

KAY. What was she finding so funny?

ADAM. She told me this would happen! "Someday that little girl will be all grown up and you'll have missed her." And she was right. Good for Rosie.

KAY. Adam ... It's not too late.

ADAM. Oh, I think it is. I've always known that Anna and I had to struggle for conversation a little, I didn't mind. When it was just Anna and me, we were both outsiders, you know? Trying to get in. But Anna and another ... that makes me the outsider. That makes *me* the stranger. *(Beat.)* On the way here I kept thinking, "I should feel young again. Finally, no dependents." But I swear to God I feel a thousand years old.

KAY. You're not a thousand years old, you're a thousand different ages. We all are. Right now you look just the same as when we first met. A frightened man in his twenties.

ADAM. You're hallucinating. What kind of drugs have they got you on, anyway?

KAY. You were running from Anna just like now. You said you

needed a break from the screaming. I said, "Colonel, you're hilarious. Your country needs you and you shoulder the burden. Your family needs you and you head to the nearest bar."

ADAM. *(Irritated.)* Look, don't blame me, Kay. I make the effort. What the hell do you think these dinners are about? Why the hell do you think I fly into New York every time I have to report to D.C. even though I hate New York! She hates Texas, so I never ask her to come to Texas. It's me that makes the effort! I have been making the effort for years! I show up at the overpriced hellhole that she's picked and I sit there! *(Beat.)*

KAY. Don't show up at four in the morning, ask for my help and then yell at me. I am not a wife. *(Beat.)* It's not too late.

ADAM. It is too late. Rosie was right. I missed her. She passed me by.

KAY. If she passed you by, you know what to do.

ADAM. No. I don't.

KAY. For God's sakes man, give chase!

Scene 7

An art gallery

Anna and Helena staring at incomprehensibly abstract modern art.

Eventually Helena begins to study Anna instead.

HELENA. Miss Anna? You are totally wearing a little outfit.

ANNA. What do you mean?

HELENA. You're wearing a little scarf.

ANNA. So?

HELENA. Your bag matches your shoes.

ANNA. Are you complimenting me?

HELENA. I am complimenting you, absolutely I am. You look incredible.

ANNA. Thanks.

HELENA. When did you become such a *woman?* When did you

become such an adult lady? I mean, maybe it's that I haven't seen you in a while, but you look so different. I mean you always look beautiful but right now what I'm getting, what you're projecting, what I'm picking up, is that you are an adult suddenly. You look great. You look really put together.

ANNA. Thanks.

HELENA. You look like the kind of lady I have no business knowing. You look like the kind of lady who has stocks.

ANNA. I do have some stocks.

HELENA. *(Flabbergasted.)* From the stock market? Shares? You have shares in things?

ANNA. Sure.

HELENA. What stocks do you have?

ANNA. Most of it's in environmentally friendly waste management.

HELENA. Wow. I am a child. Do you think I'm like a child?

ANNA. No.

HELENA. Really? Even though I dress like a clown?

ANNA. I like how you dress.

HELENA. I'm just so used to seeing you in jeans. Where did these dresses come from all of a sudden? Is it Sean? Does he prefer you in dresses?

ANNA. He's never commented one way or the other.

HELENA. Oh really? He doesn't care what you wear?

ANNA. I don't think so.

HELENA. That's nice. It's so long since I've been in a relationship that I can't remember what it's like. Somehow, in my imagination, the guy says, "You must wear *this,* woman! Now suck my cock!" but that's not what it's like, right? That's just my fucked-up imagination. Honestly, secretly, I think I'm terrified of men. Even like, with my brother sometimes, he'll be talking to me and all I'll be thinking is, "You have a penis, you have a penis," and I find it *terrifying.* You know what I mean?

ANNA. Kind of …

HELENA. No, but it's so great about you and Sean. You seem so happy.

ANNA. I am.

HELENA. That's great. Isn't it amazing how we find each other? Like him being Irish and a personal trainer, I mean, that's crazy! He's from Ireland!

ANNA. I know.

HELENA. And a personal trainer! I would never have thought in a million years that you — or in fact anyone I know — could find a meaningful relationship with a personal trainer. But you have. *(Beat.)* Do you guys have sex all the time?

ANNA. No.

HELENA. And you said it was really good, right. You said the sex was good.

ANNA. Sure.

HELENA. Can you see me with a boyfriend? Can you see that in my future?

ANNA. Of course.

HELENA. That's good. Sometimes I find I can't ... *(Her voice starts to break a little, tears close.)* picture it as closely as I used to. The only guys that like me are married, or gay. The last time little Helena actually had full-blown sex, it turned out the guy was married. Anyhow, let's talk about you, we always talk about me, let's talk about you. You want to?

ANNA. Sure ...

HELENA. Talk. I'll listen.

ANNA. Something weird happened last night. My dad telephoned. Just, he said, to *chat*. I have never heard him use the word chat in his life.

HELENA. Right, you guys don't chat, you have awkward conversations twice a year.

ANNA. Exactly.

HELENA. So how was chatting?

ANNA. It was ridiculous. We have nothing to chat about. Normally I hide that by never shutting up. I saw a fascinating movie I say, I'll say. A student came to me with a fascinating problem. I'm always trying to fascinate him. And I don't think I've ever fascinated him once.

HELENA. God, that's so sad.

ANNA. I know. All I do is try to entertain him.

HELENA. Like a geisha.

ANNA. Right. But on the phone, last night, I didn't. There was a lot of silence. *(Beat.)* I didn't tell him the big news.

HELENA. What's the big news?

ANNA. Another publisher passed on my book.

HELENA. *What?* What is wrong with these people?

ANNA. Nobody is interested in Keats' punctuation. I should have

30

seen that coming, really. I mean I wasn't even interested half the time I was writing it, I wanted to write about Emily Dickenson's punctuation, remember, but then Simon said everyone wrote about Emily Dickenson's punctuation and I just happened to be reading Keats at the time, and now it's five fucking years later and my whole life has been about Keats' punctuation and it looks like it was a waste of time.

HELENA. If no one wants to publish your book, that just confirms that it's frickin' excellent. It's a topsy-turvy universe. If something is worthless, we raise it up. Something of value, we trample it into the frickin' mud.

ANNA. It's the title, Sean thinks. It's the fucking title. *Keats' Punctuation.*

HELENA. Did Sean also tell you that you're a genius and that your book is brilliant?

ANNA. He hasn't read it.

HELENA. What?

ANNA. I told him not to. It would bore him.

HELENA. But you wrote it.

ANNA. But it's not for everybody. Which is why they won't publish it. *(Beat.)* What?

HELENA. I just don't see how you can be with someone who doesn't want to read your work.

ANNA. He read a chapter, I think.

HELENA. *(Shocked.)* How could he only read a chapter of it? It's your brain, it's your heart, it's your soul, how can he — I don't even *know* Sean. I find it really weird that you've been seeing each other forever and I've met him like five times. Does he even like me?

ANNA. Of course he does.

HELENA. Because I kind of got the impression that he didn't like me.

ANNA. When?

HELENA. You remember how I was telling the story about how I got really drunk at my dad's sixtieth birthday party and cried and kind of ruined it for everybody and he just seemed really judgmental.

ANNA. I don't think he was judging you. He was just listening.

HELENA. Even you said he was judgmental, remember. Didn't you tell me that on your first date he totally judged you for being in therapy?

ANNA. I was wrong. That was — that was about something else.

HELENA. You never tell me anything about him.

ANNA. What is it that you want to know?

HELENA. I don't *know*, you just never talk about him.

ANNA. Because there's nothing to say.

HELENA. That can't be true. He's such a huge part of your life! And I totally feel you making him separate!

ANNA. I'm not.

HELENA. Yes you *are!*

ANNA. He works all the time. I work all the time. The little time we have together we want to spend by ourselves. And if I don't talk about him, it's because I have nothing to say about him except that I *love* him. And he makes me happy. And it makes you unhappy when I'm happy.

HELENA. I can't believe you would think that.

ANNA. We start talking about me being happy and within ten minutes you're in tears because you're not happy as well. You and me like to talk about our problems. Sean's not a problem, so I don't want to talk about him. No one wants to publish my fucking book, let's talk about that. My dad is calling me on the phone and acting crazy, let's talk about that! This exhibition is horrifying, let's talk about that. But leave Sean alone!

HELENA. Wow. I had no idea you felt this way. Thank you for telling me. This is very enlightening. *(Pause.)* Maybe I do cry a lot because guess what, big surprise, little ol' Helena is an emotional person — but I think I am also a very joyful person —

ANNA. You are ...

HELENA. I am a person of extremes, but do not tell me that I am incapable of celebrating with you. Do not tell me I am the person who can only discuss misery.

ANNA. Not just miserable things. Deep things! Like ... art ... and ... you know ... Deep things!

HELENA. But you're in love, Anna! Isn't love deep?

ANNA. It's private. It's private right now. *(Pause.)*

HELENA. But you're happy. And the sex is wonderful.

ANNA. Sometimes we have sex and it's wonderful. Sometimes I never felt more alone in my life.

Scene 8

A gym, Dublin, Ireland

Max, sweating, exhausted, is on the running machine. Sean stands next to him.

MAX. This woman you're seeing ...
SEAN. Anna.
MAX. Do you torture her like this?
SEAN. She has no interest.
MAX. Been going on for some time now, hasn't it? *(No response from Sean.)* When are we going to meet her? Does she not want to visit this marvelous country of ours?
SEAN. Oh she does. Very much.
MAX. So?
SEAN. I'll never bring a girl home again unless it's to ask her to marry me.
MAX. It must be about that time, isn't that right?
SEAN. According to whose timetable?
MAX. Well, how serious is it? What are you doing? *(Sean speeds up the machine. Max runs.)* Isn't this just a metaphor for life? You sweat and you strain and you still end up in the same place. This is giving me an existential crisis! *(Running faster.)* You're a fucking torturer. I had no idea. I had no idea that torturing people was your fucking career of choice ... Vanity. One of the seven deadly sins. A man my age is supposed to spread a little.
SEAN. You'd find this easier if you would just shut up.
MAX. I think I might die. Soon. In the next five minutes. I feel it. My death approaches. He's at my back. You're killing your uncle, Sean. Your own flesh and blood. This can't be healthy.
SEAN. It is.
MAX. But I'm about to throw up.
SEAN. You're doing great.
MAX. Oh, you're just feeding me your personal trainer bullshit. I'm not an American, Sean. I don't believe I'm the best fucker in

the world just because somebody tells me so!

SEAN. Alright, what about this. You're a heart attack waiting to happen! And when you're dead, Auntie Millie will say, "That lazy bastard. I could have had him for another fifteen years if only he exercised more."

MAX. Fifteen years?

SEAN. Now you know what you're chasing after. *(Pause. Max runs, more determined.)* A few more seconds now …

MAX. Fuck you! This is bullshit! This is a terrible way to spend time!

SEAN. Ten, nine, eight, seven …

MAX. I hate you, Sean, I hate you, Sean!

SEAN. Five, four …

MAX. Fuck you! Fuck me! Fuck everybody!

SEAN. And now we slow down to walking … *(Sean slows the machine down to a fast walk.)*

MAX. We don't stop?

SEAN. No. We get our heart rate down, we get our breath back, but we keep going …

MAX. "We" nothing! What are you doing? You get paid for this shit?

SEAN. I do.

MAX. I'm going to be in pain tomorrow, aren't I? This is the last walking I'll be doing for quite some time, isn't that right?

SEAN. Got to push through the pain, Max.

MAX. Listen to you … like a fucking Marine …

SEAN. You're doing great.

MAX. I am not doing great! I am pathetic. The seventeen-year-old Max is watching and he is in tears.

SEAN. You really are doing well.

MAX. What happened to great? *(His breath is steadier now.)* So this girl you've been seeing. We were talking about whether or not it was serious.

SEAN. Her name is Anna.

MAX. Well, you're on the other side of the world, Sean! We've never met her! She's not quite real to us, you know what I mean? Your mother's worried you're keeping her away deliberately.

SEAN. Why?

MAX. She thinks you're ashamed of where you're from.

SEAN. That's ridiculous.

MAX. She gets the impression that Anna is a different sort of per-son, a posh sort of person. Teaches at a university, doesn't she? Your mother would feel better if she met her, that's all. But if it's not going to last —

SEAN. I didn't say it wasn't going to last.

MAX. Well, two years, boy! When I was your age, I had two kids already! The time goes by quick, what are you waiting for? A sign from God? If she's not the right fish, throw her back in the sea.

SEAN. How do I know?

MAX. How do you know? Do you love her?

SEAN. Aye.

MAX. No, but do you really love her, do you truly love her? No, don't make me run! *(But Sean has stopped the machine. Max sees Sean looking very serious.)* What? What's the matter with you? *(A beat.)* What, Sean?

SEAN. I don't know. She wants to move in together. I don't want to. And if I don't want to, then I should end it. But I don't want to end it. I'm a dick. I don't know what I'm doing. She probably wants to have babies. And I'm just … I don't know what to do! I don't want to be the bad guy! But I don't want to end it! But I *should* end it because I'm a liar!

MAX. Who are you lying to?

SEAN. To Anna! I'm lying next to her at night and against my will, against my fucking will, there's this other girl in my head and I'm thinking that I love her. Or that I loved her. I loved her more.

MAX. Who?

SEAN. Rachel. *(Beat.)* Christ, Max. I'm asleep with one woman, I'm dreaming of another.

MAX. I haven't done enough for you, Sean. You had no dad and I've tried to look out for you but with four of my own and …

SEAN. Max —

MAX. Let me finish. I've been remiss in my responsibilities towards you. A kid needs a father. You need a father, this moment right here is why a child needs a father. Let me be yours. For this moment, let me be yours.

SEAN. Alright.

MAX. Son. You will always think of other women. *(Beat.)* I do, even now. Helen May.

SEAN. You've not been remiss, Max. You had your own family.

MAX. But you are my family.

SEAN. I'm alright.

MAX. I don't know how you did it, but you've grown up fine. *(Beat.)*

SEAN. So who was Helen May then?

MAX. It was with her that I had my first kiss. Beautiful girl. Became a nun.

SEAN. I see you had quite an effect on her.

MAX. We were kids. Running around the playground. The girls would make daisy chains and chase the boys. If they put the chain around their necks, they had to kiss them. And us boys, off we ran. We ran, but we wanted to be caught. Helen May caught me. So we turned and we faced each other. And I bent forward like I was bowing, you know? And we were making these little Chinese bows at each other. And I closed my eyes and she kissed me. Oh, it was delicious. Some nights, Millie is asleep, and I pretend that I seek out Helen May in her nunnery. I call up to the tower! Helen, do you remember me? Run away with me! Millie gives a little snort and awakes. "I can't sleep," I tell her. "Well, think about Helen May," she says. "That usually drops you off." *(Beat.)*

SEAN. *(Surprised.)* She doesn't mind it?

MAX. She doesn't mind.

Scene 9

Lecture theater, Columbia University

Adam alone. Awkward. Out of place. The outskirts of a party. Helena arrives, hurried. She looks disheveled. Adam is relieved to see someone he knows.

ADAM. Helena!

HELENA. Hey … how are you? Gosh, it's been … .

ADAM. A long time.

HELENA. Can you believe it? She's totally published! Awesome! Where is she? *(Adam nods offstage.)* The woman of the hour.

ADAM. I'm just letting her do her thing.

HELENA. How long are you in town for?

ADAM. Just a couple of hours. The timing was off for me.

HELENA. That's so amazing that you flew in!

ADAM. Wouldn't miss it.

HELENA. I'm late-a-roony. I decided to have a catnap and it turned into a sleeporama. I have very vivid dreams, you know, and I was just having this crazy dream that I — *(Sean comes over.)*
SEAN. Helena. How are you?
HELENA. Honestly, I hate being asked that. People just want you to say fine. It's a lot of pressure. There's so much pressure to be *unreal* with people, you know?
SEAN. Okay ...
HELENA. Okay.
SEAN. *(To Adam.)* Anna told me to check on you. She's in the middle of a very dry conversation about ellipses.
HELENA. Ellipses are fascinating, actually.
ADAM. I don't even know what they are.
HELENA. They're the little dot-dot-dot at the end of a sentence. They change everything. For actors.
ADAM. Helena, what are you working on now? *(A long pause. Gradually it dawns on Adam that Helena will not be answering his question.)*
HELENA. Is there any wine at this shindig?
SEAN. Over there. *(Helena exits towards wine. Pause.)* Work going well for you, Adam?
ADAM. Very well. *(Beat.)* And yours? Work?
SEAN. Great. Fine. *(Beat.)* I've been taking a class in karate. I might incorporate it into some of the training.
ADAM. I have a black belt in karate.
SEAN. Anna told me. You could give me a few pointers, maybe.
ADAM. When I was taught, the object was to kill the other person. Different kind of training. *(The ensuing silence is broken by the screech of a microphone. Then we hear Simon's amplified voice. All our attention is on Adam and Sean's reactions.)*
SIMON. *(Offstage.)* Welcome everybody, welcome. I won't take up much of your time, I just want to say how pleased we are to host this event tonight. Anna — *(Adam and Sean listen, pride on their faces.)* began life as an undergrad here at Columbia. No actually, she began life as a baby. My little joke. Sorry. *(Adam and Sean are unimpressed.)* Anna began her *academic* life at Columbia as an undergraduate and I actually had the pleasure of teaching her ... she was everything you want a student to be, quick, attentive, studious, curious, passionate. *(Pride on Adam and Sean's faces. They even smile at each other.)* Anna went on to get her Ph.D. here,

and to my great delight she and I became more than student and teacher ... *(Adam and Sean tense, horrified.)* we became colleagues. *(Adam and Sean relax.)* Tonight, we are here to celebrate the book that bloomed from her Ph.D. thesis. *The Grammar of Love: Keats and Punctuation* represents Anna's first academic publication. It's really wonderful and without a doubt one of the most exciting publications to have come out of Columbia all *year*. So, Anna, if you'd like to come up here and say a few words? *(Helena walks up to Adam and Sean. We hear Anna's voice through the microphone.)*

ANNA. Thanks everyone for coming ... I want to thank Simon especially for so much help with the book and the faculty for all of their support and my dad for flying all the way in from Texas and my boyfriend for putting up with me and ... you know ... thanks for coming...! Drink up! *(Screech. The microphone is switched off. Adam and Sean are modestly delighted with their acknowledgement.)*

SEAN. *(To Helena.)* After this, I thought we'd get a drink downtown. I hate student bars.

ADAM. Anna's mother would have been incredibly proud of her. She always hoped to write a book herself.

HELENA. Everyone has a novel in them, right?

ADAM. She never had the discipline to get it out. *(Anna enters.)*

ANNA. *(Tense.)* That was a horrible speech.

SEAN. No.

ADAM. Short, quick and to the point.

SEAN. You thanked everyone you needed to thank and then you got off the stage. *(Helena bursts into tears and runs offstage.)*

ADAM. What's the matter with her?

SEAN. This isn't about the dog again, is it?

ADAM. The what?

SEAN. Her dog died a hundred years ago. She's still in mourning.

ANNA. It's because I didn't thank her. She read the book three times and I didn't thank her. I should have thanked her ...

SEAN. That's ridiculous.

ANNA. I meant to, I, just, I was flustered.

SEAN. You've thanked her *in* the book. It's fine.

ANNA. That's why she's crying. Bet you.

SEAN. *(Angry.)* Then she can get over it. Jesus, it's your night.

ANNA. Some night. Could it be any more anti-climactic? Five years of work and this is what I get? Wine, cheese, and a lecture theatre. There's still equations left up on the blackboard, for fuck's sake. Sorry, Dad.

ADAM. Come now. *(Beat.)* Come now.

ANNA. Yeah, well, now I have to write another one. It never ends. *(Beat.)* I better see if Helena's alright —

SEAN. *Leave* her ... It's your night. *(Beat.)*

ANNA. *(To Sean.)* I am so fucking sick of her — *(To Adam.)* sorry Dad — *(To Sean.)* I swear to God it's the one night that's meant to be about me and she dragged me to one side and started telling me her dream, and when the head of the faculty came over to introduce me to some donor or something, she acted really ... you know ... mad. Like she was mad that the story of her *dream* got interrupted. I mean for God's sake ...

ADAM. *(Emphatically.)* She has *aged.* I almost didn't recognize her. How's her acting going?

SEAN. She never works.

ADAM. Didn't you take me to see a play she was in?

ANNA. Ages ago.

ADAM. I thought she was *excellent.*

ANNA. She was.

ADAM. *Really* talented, I thought.

ANNA. What time's your flight?

ADAM. I've got about an hour still.

ANNA. You should go now. Get some food. You can't eat cheese for dinner. I have to stay for the end. I'm sorry it's such a pathetic little gathering, Dad. I told you it wasn't worth flying in for. Oh Jesus, I'm being waved over. *(To Sean.)* Come with. *(They walk off. Adam alone. He's almost relieved to see a tear-stained Helena.)*

ADAM. Are you okay?

HELENA. Oh, fine. I cry all the time. *(Beat.)* You know, I just woke up, I had a really intense dream so ...

ADAM. I just remembered. Last time I saw you I was here. You were doing a show with the students.

HELENA. *Midsummer Night's Dream.*

ADAM. That's right! You played Bottom!

HELENA. Right ...

ADAM. You were excellent. *(Beat.)* I have to go. It was good to see you, Helena. *(He leaves.)*

HELENA. *(To the audience.)* I had this dream that I passed a store front and there were Jell-Os in the window. I went inside. There

39

was a back room full of children. My dad was there. He was playing with them. I said, surprised, "What are you doing here, Dad?" He was confused, like he didn't understand the question. He was playing cards with a little girl so I let him be. I started talking to a serious little boy. The boy told me he'd tried to kill himself that morning. He told me all the children there had tried to die. And then I remembered that I had tried to kill myself the day before. That's why my dad was there. He was there for me.

Scene 10

Acadia National Park, Maine

Sean and Rachel sitting on a bench. A cold, blowy day.

RACHEL. Smoke?
SEAN. Gave up.
RACHEL. You always were a goody two shoes.
SEAN. Set a good example for my clients. You know.
RACHEL. How'd you find me?
SEAN. Facebook.
RACHEL. You're not on Facebook.
SEAN. I had to join it to find you.
RACHEL. I looked for you there when I joined. But I figured it wasn't very you.
SEAN. So you didn't mind me getting in touch?
RACHEL. No, why should I?
SEAN. Never pegged you for a country girl.
RACHEL. I'm not really.
SEAN. You're married.
RACHEL. Yes.
SEAN. Not a question. Facebook. Tells you everything, really. So much stuff. I had no idea. I had no idea. Ten minutes after I joined, three ex-girlfriends in Ireland wanted to know what I was up to. Sending me quizzes to find out which Golden Girl I'm most like. *(Beat.)* Rose, by the way. *(Beat.)* I shut my page down already.

(Beat.) Anyway, sorry, who'd you marry?

RACHEL. His name's Devrak.

SEAN. What is it?

RACHEL. Devrak. He's from India.

SEAN. I didn't know there were Indian people in Maine.

RACHEL. Had you ever seriously thought about it?

SEAN. No.

RACHEL. What about you? Married? Girlfriend?

SEAN. Girlfriend.

RACHEL. What's her name?

SEAN. Anna.

RACHEL. Serious?

SEAN. Yup.

RACHEL. Where are you working now?

SEAN. Freelance now.

RACHEL. Still saving to run your own gym?

SEAN. Yes.

RACHEL. You always said it would take years.

SEAN. I was right.

RACHEL. I'm a — oh, you already know ... Facebook.

SEAN. You're a hairdresser.

RACHEL. Stylist.

SEAN. You never did go back to school, then?

RACHEL. No. *(Beat.)* I like cutting hair. I don't talk enough. My boss always tells me to be more chatty. But my regulars, that's what they like about me.

SEAN. That's funny.

RACHEL. What is?

SEAN. That's what my boss used to tell me. That's what I'd tell him.

RACHEL. I think that's why we liked to drink so much together. Loosened our lips.

SEAN. I drink less now.

RACHEL. I was A.A. all the way, baby. A.A. I don't miss any of it. Half the people in my band are in recovery.

SEAN. *(Pleased.)* You're still playing?

RACHEL. Oh yes. We have kind of a following here in Maine. We're what they call "Maimous."

SEAN. How are your parents?

RACHEL. Good. Very good. Retired. I don't know where they are half the time. They bought an RV, travel up and down the country.

SEAN. I remember them saying they'd do that someday.

RACHEL. Someday's here. *(Pause. Sean begins to cry.)*

SEAN. I miss you. I still miss you. It doesn't go away. Don't say anything back. The last time I saw you, you had tubes coming out of your fucking nose. There were fucking sirens.

RACHEL. I'm sorry.

SEAN. *(Getting himself back together.)* I hate the sound of sirens. Can't stand hospitals. You know who else I think of all the time? Your folks. They hate my guts, I bet.

RACHEL. They don't think about you.

SEAN. I'll never forget your dad screaming at me in the hospital. He hit me. Did you know that? Or tried to. I jumped back. I wish I hadn't now. I wish he'd hit me hard in the face, sometimes I pretend he did. If I can't sleep, I imagine him hitting me again and again.

RACHEL. He shouldn't have done that. It wasn't your fault. You had every right to dump me.

SEAN. Dump you, hook up with you, dump you, hook up with you, and on and on and on ... I was a fucking idiot.

RACHEL. Young love. That's what it looks like.

SEAN. I'm so sorry about it.

RACHEL. You don't need to be. It really had nothing to do with you.

SEAN. Oh please —

RACHEL. It didn't. It had to do with me. Honey, back then I was drinking a bottle of vodka a day.

SEAN. I didn't know that.

RACHEL. Well, I was. I was a time bomb. That's what my lady said.

SEAN. Your what?

RACHEL. They make you see a shrink if you try to kill yourself. I was a train wreck back then.

SEAN. Not to me.

RACHEL. Yes, to you. That's why you kept dumping me!

SEAN. I don't remember. I don't remember why I broke it off. I keep asking myself why.

RACHEL. What you said was ... we need to grow up. *(Pause.)* Does your girlfriend know you came?

SEAN. Her suggestion. She said — she kept using this stupid word.

RACHEL. What word?

SEAN. It doesn't matter. It's silly.

RACHEL. What word?

SEAN. Traumatized. *(Pause.)* What did your lady say about me?

RACHEL. Not much. We talked about my family mostly.

SEAN. Oh. *(Pause.)*

RACHEL. But she said when I think of you, and I do think of you, it's just a fantasy of escape. The Sean I think of doesn't exist anymore. He's gone. And the Rachel you're thinking of doesn't exist either. Not really. She's long gone. *(Pause.)*

SEAN. I don't exist?

RACHEL. Neither do I.

Scene 11

Adam's house, Texas

Christmas Eve. Anna holds a notebook. Adam studies her. Very anxious.

ADAM. I don't know what to say. Do you want to call Sean? What can I do? Anna? I don't know what to say ... *(Anna hurls the notebook at Adam who has to dodge to avoid it.)*

ANNA. You can stop staying *that!*

ADAM. Hey!

ANNA. Asshole!

ADAM. Do you want to call Sean?

ANNA. Why would I want to call Sean?

ADAM. To comfort you ...

ANNA. God, I hate you! I have worked so hard not to hate you and now I give up. I hate you.

ADAM. I haven't done anything! I didn't even know she kept a journal!

ANNA. Of course not! Apparently you paid her no attention at all!

ADAM. I don't know what she wrote in there, but obviously it's just one-half of the truth. The truth exists between two opposing viewpoints, don't forget that, don't ever forget that.

ANNA. Patronizing. She said you were patronizing. She captured you perfectly. And I've been ignoring —

ADAM. What? No —

ANNA. — Ignoring who you really were because I thought it was her, that it was her death that made you —

ADAM. Anna ...

ANNA. She hated you!

ADAM. No! Not always.

ANNA. And you let me believe that it was a love story!

ADAM. It was! It ... Anna, you're not ...

ANNA. What?

ADAM. *(Angry.)* Will you let me think? Will you just let me think? *(Beat.)* I have sensed from you a misunderstanding about the nature of the marriage for some time now and ... *You* tell me how I was supposed to *correct* something like that? You got it all built up in your head. Not to blame you, not to blame you, but you must see that ... Anna, every couple has their problems, you're a big girl now, you know that. I'm sure you and Sean have your problems, it doesn't mean ... Please don't be so upset ... Jesus Christ, Anna! I didn't know it was up there! I kept all her things in case you wanted to go through them someday! If I thought there was anything in there that would have upset you, I would have burned it! As would she! *(Uselessly completing his sentence.)* Have ... I know she wasn't happy. There was a period where she was not happy. Neither was I. Is that what upsets you? What did she write? How unhappy was she?

ANNA. Read it!

ADAM. Anna, it was a different time, it was a difficult time, men and women spoke to each other in different ways. Anna, will you look at me, please? Let's talk about this. I don't want this to ... please do not let this ... I have been trying very hard to ... It's Christmas Eve. Come on now. This is our first Christmas together for a long time, and it's supposed to be ... we were having a very nice time, I thought ... and Sean is flying in for New Year's. This is supposed to be a new fucking era or whatever. Jesus! Why is it always like this! Why is it always such a fucking drama?

ANNA. What?

ADAM. Everything! Why does everything always turn into such a fucking drama! You're just like your mother, you know that? You're just like her right now. I want calm. Let's just calm down.

ANNA. "Adam is so distant from me, I can't bear it. Why did I marry a stone?" She wanted a divorce? You wanted a divorce? And then she got cancer and died? *That's* the story of my mother? Do not touch me!

Don't you touch me! She says she thinks you cheated on her. Did you?

ADAM. We both screwed around.

ANNA. *(Broken.)* With who? *(Beat.)*

ADAM. *(Very nervous.)* There was this one woman —

ANNA. *(Panic.)* I don't want to hear it.

ADAM. For God's sake, Anna! We weren't saints. Your mother in particular was an extremely free spirit. I don't know what period of time that journal covers but … We did love each other. And we loved you. And you didn't hear the fights because we fought in the yard. I did grieve. I don't know what she wrote about me, but I tried. I really did. It just … I was away so much. And at the beginning, when I came home … food on the table and pretty dresses … Everyone was a homemaker in Texas. I got offered a post in Japan. I wanted very much to take it. I thought it would be good for you. See the world. Learn Japanese. What a wonderful childhood, I thought. Your mother refused. That was the beginning of a coldness. And something got broken. No more pretty dresses. Suddenly not a happy woman, not a happy woman, suddenly. Suddenly she wants more. More than the house, more than the baby. And then the eighties, the nineteen-eighties … When I first served, women weren't even allowed in active combat. Now … And they're good at it! It's the darndest thing. Rosie used to tell me, "There's not so much difference between a man and a woman." I laughed in her face. And now. What do I see? In combat, with a gun, the one could be the other! And she told me all this. She told me years ago. I was limited. Anna, I admit it. I limited her. I see that now. But we were kids! You're in your thirties, you and Sean are only moving in together now! Please don't take this so hard.

ANNA. I'm packing my bags and I'm going to the airport and I'm waiting for a flight home.

ADAM. Don't do that …

ANNA. I thought the reason you were so cold and distant was because you were crippled with grief. But I was wrong. You're just cold and distant. I've put so much energy into trying to reach you. Being early to our dinners. Dressing up for you. Always trying to entertain you. No point. She married a stone.

ADAM. Anna!

Scene 12

A psychiatric ward, NYC

Helena in an enormous hospital gown. Sean, visiting her.

SEAN. How are you?

HELENA. That's a joke, right?

SEAN. Right. *(Beat.)* I brought you some books and some magazines and stuff.

HELENA. Thanks.

SEAN. Although I see they're not short on board games here. *(Beat.)* And this is chicken soup and some chicken sandwiches. I thought the food here would probably be pretty awful.

HELENA. You made these?

SEAN. Yes. I cook.

HELENA. I forgot. Anna said. You're really good at it.

SEAN. Anna doesn't eat enough. Always picking at things. Works too much. *(Beat.)* She wanted to be here. I was the one who told her to wait until I'd checked on you. Her plane had only just landed there when she got your message.

HELENA. Where's she gone this time?

SEAN. Some conference in France. She's giving a paper.

HELENA. She travels all the time now.

SEAN. Yup. I've barely seen her since we moved in together.

HELENA. She's busy, busy, busy. I had to talk to a psychiatrist this morning so that he could medicate me. I'm currently medicated, I don't know if you can tell. And he said I simply have too much time on my hands. As simple as that. Simple, simple, simple. I said to him, "Are you saying that if I worked in a bank none of this would be happening?" And do you know what he said? "I'd put money on it." And I said, "Then you'd lose your money, Doc, because if I worked in a bank then I *would* kill myself."

SEAN. They are going to let you out again, right?

HELENA. Exactly. I checked myself into rehab but I can't check myself out. I have to be released into somebody's care. My mom is driving up from Arlington. Tomorrow.

SEAN. Don't you hate your mom?

HELENA. Yes.

SEAN. That doesn't sound like a good plan.

HELENA. I don't have a fucking plan. I have to be released into someone's care.

SEAN. What about me and Anna?

HELENA. What about you?

SEAN. There's our care.

HELENA. It's too much.

SEAN. It's fine.

HELENA. No. It's too much. I should go home. My parents have money. They can pay to get me some ... whatever it is I need ...

SEAN. I'm free all day. If you want company.

HELENA. What will we talk about?

SEAN. Did Anna tell you about the journal?

HELENA. Her mom's journal? Uh-huh.

SEAN. She won't talk about it. She's gone silent. Like a ghost.

HELENA. That's how she was when I first met her. Like a ghost. Her mom had just died. She appeared at boarding school. A mystery. Never said a word to anyone.

SEAN. How did you get her to open up? She said you guys used to talk to each other after lights were out, that she'd cry in your arms.

HELENA. I asked her lots of questions, I guess. I don't really remember. We were both always the last people picked for softball. It was a common bond.

SEAN. I ask her questions. She says she doesn't want to talk about it.

HELENA. Push her. You have to push her. (Sean sighs.)

SEAN. Sorry. You don't want to hear about our problems.

HELENA. I do. It's comforting. What's the worst thing? What's the worst thing about where you guys are at right now?

SEAN. The not knowing. Not knowing if we're going to end up together. We've been together so long and we're totally lost.

HELENA. That sounds awful.

SEAN. It's like floating on a sea, scanning the horizon for land and you know it's out there but ... No plan. It feels like we're drifting. In the land of not-knowing.

HELENA. That's where I live.

SEAN. Hi.

HELENA. Hi.

Scene 13

A hospital bed, D.C.

Kay's propped up but her eyes are closed. Somewhere a machine beeps. Adam watches her. Silence for a while, then ...

KAY. Just, Christ, say something. Don't just sit there and watch me die.

ADAM. I thought you fell asleep.

KAY. No, I didn't, although with your conversation I might as well have.

ADAM. I'm sorry.

KAY. Talk. Tell me something classified. Come on. My lips are sealed. I'll take it to the grave.

ADAM. The government was responsible for 9/11.

KAY. Really?

ADAM. No.

KAY. *(Amused.)* You're such an asshole. *(Pause.)*

ADAM. Are you in pain?

KAY. There's no pain. They've got me on all sorts of wonderful things. The only problem is I'll be asleep any second. I drop off, just like that.

ADAM. That's okay. I'm here for a while. I took a few weeks off.

KAY. Why did you do that?

ADAM. Why do you think?

KAY. I haven't got a few weeks.

ADAM. Who knows with you? You're a miracle.

KAY. Not anymore.

ADAM. Always.

KAY. I don't want you here. Getting mushy.

ADAM. I won't —

KAY. I'm going out of this world the way I came in. All by myself. That's the way I want it. And don't you feel sad, or bad, or anything. I'm off to see the end of the world. *(Adam tries to control his emotions.)* How's Anna? Give me a final installment.

48

ADAM. Barely talking to me. I told her I was coming East but ... it's probably just a coincidence, but she had to go to a conference. Toronto. She's been giving a lot of papers this year. Doing incredibly well.

KAY. At least you skipped New York. That must have made you happy.

ADAM. No, no. I flew into New York anyway. Saw Sean. Gave him another karate lesson. He's a good man, a very good man. He's clearly devoted to her. Rosie would have approved, he's very much a new man. He does nearly all of the cooking, he told me. Loves to cook.

KAY. He sounds like quite a guy.

ADAM. He is. I really think he is.

KAY. I'm glad. I always wanted everything to work out great for her. It had to be so tough losing her mother like that. *(Beat.)* I don't even know what she looks like.

ADAM. Would you like to meet her?

KAY. What, real, live, in person?

ADAM. Yes.

KAY. I thought she wasn't talking to you.

ADAM. I could try.

KAY. I don't need to meet her. I like thinking of her knocking them dead in Toronto with a man in her kitchen waiting for her to come home.

ADAM. But I'd like you to meet her.

KAY. Too late.

ADAM. Do you want to see a photograph? *(He gets a book out of his bag — Anna's book. Anna's picture is on the dust jacket.)*

KAY. That her? This her book?

ADAM. Yes.

KAY. Boy. Weighs a ton.

ADAM. I know.

KAY. You can tell her sometime that when she dyed her hair blue, I was the one who told you to get over it. *(Beat.)* Now get her book off my chest before it stops my heart completely. *(Adam takes the book.)*

ADAM. Can I hold your hand?

KAY. What do you think? *(Long pause. He takes her hand.)*

Scene 14

Anna and Helena on the telephone

Helena is calling. She's in North Carolina.

ANNA. *(To Helena.)* Hey!

HELENA. Hey! I didn't think you were going to pick up.

ANNA. I just got in. How is it?

HELENA. I've moved to a town that only has seven hundred and forty people in it, how do you think it is? *(No response.)* I feel so weird being back in the *South*, because as you know I have a lot of *shame* about it ...

ANNA. Yeah, I just walked through the door. I heard your message. Your message said, "Help."

HELENA. You know what? I was trying to be funny. But I guess that's not so funny.

ANNA. It frightened me.

HELENA. Oh honey, I'm sorry. It's okay. I'm okay here. I love it. I can tell I'll love it. You know what? It is so beautiful. The trees around here, and the mountains — they are just gorgeous. And there are *stars*. You can see stars out here, Anna. I'm going over to my front door right now and ... I'm looking at stars. *(She opens her front door. Sure enough, stars. She sits down on her doorstep looking up.)*

ANNA. When does school start?

HELENA. Tomorrow. A lecture. "Fundamentals of Massage: The Science of Touch."

ANNA. The *science* of touch. I like it.

HELENA. How are you?

ANNA. Working like crazy.

HELENA. How's Sean?

ANNA. Fine.

HELENA. Just fine?

ANNA. Yeah.

HELENA. So you guys are great?

ANNA. I'm worried I want to break up with him.

HELENA. Huh ...

ANNA. I catch myself imagining he's having sex with someone else and I burst in and then I'm allowed. I'm allowed to leave him. The other day I was teaching and I suddenly imagined he had cancer, he was dying, and I was happy! Because then I could meet somebody else. I feel like I'm going to throw up.

HELENA. Are you okay? Anna?

ANNA. It's just ... my heart's pounding.

HELENA. Are you sitting down?

ANNA. No.

HELENA. Sit down. And breathe. *(Beat.)* Are you sitting down? Are you breathing?

ANNA. I actually feel like I'm going to have a panic attack ...

HELENA. Honey? Are you sitting?

ANNA. Yes! I'm sitting. Sorry.

HELENA. That's okay. *(Silence. Anna breathes.)*

ANNA. I am freaking out. I am freaking out. What if I want to break up with him?

HELENA. Can you talk? Do you think you can talk about it without having a panic attack? Or should we just stick with breathing? Because I can sit here on the other end of the phone with you and just breathe. I have got no problem with that. I have got all night.

ANNA. Everything's fine, between us, nothing's happened, it's just ... I can't bear for him to touch me. Not at the moment. I sleep pushed up against the wall.

HELENA. You don't need to make a decision about anything right now. When your body's ready to make a decision, it will make a decision. It will stay or go. You don't need to over-think it.

ANNA. Okay. I don't want to talk about it anymore, okay?

HELENA. No problemo. How's the new book coming? Emily Dickinson?

ANNA. No time to write it. People keep asking me for articles about Keats. He's become my life partner. Could I be any more fucking esoteric and obscure?

HELENA. It's not just about Keats. It's not just about grammar. It's about art. It's about indicating, right, indicating, what is it you say in your book? That "seemingly insignificant details result in beauty!" I mean, that's what you're devoting your life to! To beauty! And if we don't have beauty, then what's the point of progressing! What's the point of recovering from cancer? What's the point of anything?

ANNA. God, I love you.

Scene 15

A threshold, Ireland

Anna and Linda sit with their backsides squarely inside the house and their legs outside. Bright sunlight. Linda might wear sunglasses.

LINDA. The weather's not always like this, you know. This is very unusual weather for Ireland.

ANNA. That's what Sean said.

LINDA. You've been very lucky, weather-wise.

ANNA. Yup.

LINDA. I must say it's been a pleasure meeting you. You're very nice.

ANNA. Thank you.

LINDA. No really. You're very, very nice. I hope you'll come again.

ANNA. I hope so too.

LINDA. We've been like ships in the night, haven't we? All Seany's fault. You're a pleasure, you've been a pleasure. I was really nervous before you came, you know? I was incredibly nervous. The night before you arrived, I was up all night worrying about how to pretend to be a totally different person for a week, but then you came and I hadn't the energy and then we had a little drink and we got on fine, didn't we?

ANNA. Absolutely.

LINDA. I shall miss you.

ANNA. It's not over. There's still two more days.

LINDA. Sean will be back with the sandwiches soon. Won't he be surprised? Seeing me on the front step.

ANNA. How are you feeling?

LINDA. Fine. I feel fine. That Xanax really is something.

ANNA. I'll leave you a few.

LINDA. I would never have thought that a tiny little pill could have such a huge effect. I mean, I'm not one hundred percent, you know. I wouldn't say that. I know that I'm frightened in my head. But my heart ... steady as a rock. Incredible.

ANNA. I use them for flying.

LINDA. How do you get them?

ANNA. My friend Helena gave them to me.

LINDA. Is that legal?

ANNA. Absolutely not.

LINDA. Did your friend Helena not want to keep them for herself?

ANNA. No. Her mother, who is a psychiatrist, mails them to her. But Helena won't take them because she thinks it's her mother's way of trying to control her.

LINDA. Interesting people you know out there. *(Beat.)* I honestly can't believe I'm sitting on the step. If a neighbor walks b,y they'll shit.

ANNA. Is it people you're frightened of, or space?

LINDA. Oh, I don't know. It's that there's a world out there. *(Beat.)* The attack was so long ago, I wonder if maybe even that has nothing to do with it. Maybe I was always to end up this way. Born with a deficiency of something.

ANNA. You haven't ended up this way. It's where you are right now.

LINDA. My brother says it would have been easier on me if they'd caught him. But they never did. I was no help at all. He was all a haze to me, you see. It was a day like this, a rare day, a warm day, and I fell asleep, and by the time I woke up again the mist was coming in, the light was leaving, and ... I couldn't give the police a single detail. They said it was shock. They said he shocked all the details out of my head. My pretty little head. I overheard the doctor and that's what he said. He said, "The bastard shocked every detail out of her pretty little head."

ANNA. I can't imagine ...

LINDA. So no, he was never caught.

ANNA. Most, I believe, aren't.

LINDA. That's right. Running free. When I can't sleep, I imagine they found the one who did it. I get a telephone call. "Hello Linda," they say. "We've found him." So I go down to the station. They take me to a black room. A cell. He's chained up. Handcuffed. And they leave me alone with my man in the mist. And I walk up to his chair and I ... Oh Lord. If you knew ... you'd be amazed with the kind of things my imagination comes up with. Still. A long time ago. No need to be maudlin. *(Pause.)*

ANNA. After lunch, Sean wants to take a walk along the cliffs. He says there's no view more beautiful.

LINDA. It was always his favorite place.

ANNA. So he says.

LINDA. *(Meaningfully.)* I know he really wants to take you there. *(Beat.)* There's heather, purple for miles just about. And you walk and you walk and there's only sea ahead of you. You're standing on an edge of the world. *(Beat.)* Shall we go in, have a nice cup of tea?

ANNA. I thought you wanted Sean to see you on the step. *(Beat.)* You'll make his day. *(Beat.)* I bet Claire would do this with you, if you wanted her to. Once in a while.

LINDA. Don't get your hopes up. You're not The Miracle Worker.

ANNA. Listen, I'm an American. I am terminally optimistic. I want to you to visit us in the States.

LINDA. *(Scoffing, but pleased.)* Visit you in the States. Have we not established that I'm bat-shit crazy?

ANNA. Maybe one day you'll find yourself on a plane to America. See where we live. You've only seen a photograph of our apartment. And our apartment has only seen a photograph of you.

LINDA. A photograph?

ANNA. Sure. You're on the bookcase.

LINDA. What am I doing there?

ANNA. You're framed. *(Pause.)*

LINDA. Fresh life. That's what you are.

Scene 16

The woods of North Carolina

Helena marches, intrepid, through the woods. Finding a clearing, she stops and prepares herself and the space for meditation. Ready, she crosses her legs, closes her eyes and begins.

Enough silence to hear silence. Then a growl. The growl comes from a bear. Helena opens one eye. She sees nothing troubling. She resumes her meditation.

Behind her, Gideon enters. He has a rifle pointed beyond Helena, offstage. Helena hears Gideon's footsteps, opens her eyes again, sees the gun.

Helena offers up an earsplitting scream. Confusion.

GIDEON. Shhhh!
HELENA. What the fuck do you want? What the fuck do you want from me?
GIDEON. Ma'am … ma'am …
HELENA. I knew it! I knew that one day I'd be raped!
GIDEON. Get down on the ground. I need you to stay very quiet.
HELENA. I bet you do, you filthy son of a bitch!
GIDEON. There is a bear behind you. *(Helena whirls around and sees the bear. She screams again, even more loudly if possible and then throws herself to the ground and curls up into a tiny little ball.)*
HELENA. Oh my God, oh my God, oh my God …
GIDEON. Stay calm now …
HELENA. Is this because I have my period?
GIDEON. This is because we're walking about where bears live.
HELENA. Is he still there?
GIDEON. It's a lady bear and yes she is. She's just watching us.
HELENA. Are you going to kill her?
GIDEON. Only if she charges.

HELENA. So we just wait?

GIDEON. That's right. That's what we do for the minute. *(Beat.)*

HELENA. Now what's happening?

GIDEON. Not much. She's just looking right at you.

HELENA. At me?

GIDEON. That's what she's doing right now.

HELENA. Can I look at her?

GIDEON. Sure. Sure you can. Just don't make direct eye contact. *(From her fetal position, Helena sneaks a peek at the bear.)* You know what we're going to do? We're going to back away slowly ... *(Helena gets up, cautiously, staring at the bear.)*

HELENA. I am making eye contact ...

GIDEON. Ma'am, she's going to perceive that as a challenge —

HELENA. She's looking at me, I'm looking at her. "For I am as ugly as a bear, for beasts that meet me run away for fear." But she's not ugly. And she's not running away. *(Helena is crying. But for the first time in her life she cries tears of joy.)* You're not ugly ... *(Helena starts walking towards the bear.)*

GIDEON. Lady —

HELENA. We're not ugly ...

GIDEON. Woman, get away from that bear, she'll rip your fucking head off.

HELENA. I don't think so ... *(Gideon shoots, Helena charges him.)* No! *(She knocks Gideon to the ground, landing on top of him. This is not an un-erotic moment for either of them.)*

GIDEON. There now. She's taking off.

HELENA. Are you blind? We were communing. I was communing with her and you betrayed the *trust* —

GIDEON. No ...

HELENA. Yes.

GIDEON. I just saved your life, you crazy bitch.

HELENA. My. What happened to ma'am?

GIDEON. I just saved your life, ma'am.

HELENA. Helena.

GIDEON. Helena. Gideon.

HELENA. Nice to meet you, I suppose.

GIDEON. You were not having a moment with that bear.

HELENA. No, I was. It was quite a profound moment actually. Until you spoiled it with your gun.

GIDEON. *(Grinning.)* Are you on 'shrooms? Can I have some?

HELENA. You can make fun all you want, but I looked in her eyes and she looked into my eyes and it was ... it was life-changing, actually. I saw total acceptance. And she was feeling some —
GIDEON. Bears feel only three things. Hungry. Sleepy. And like they need to take a shit. They're a lot like men in that way.
HELENA. Oh God.
GIDEON. What?
HELENA. I hate it when men limit themselves like that. You can be so much more. You can be sensitive, and loving and complex and broken and ...
GIDEON. *(Slowly.)* I find you *fascinating* ...
HELENA. You do?
GIDEON. Where are you from?
HELENA. I was living in New York but I moved out here just a few weeks ago.
GIDEON. That's a change of pace.
HELENA. Yup.
GIDEON. Well, I've been out here fifteen years and they still call me a newcomer.
HELENA. What does that make me?
GIDEON. A baby.
HELENA. Where'd you move from?
GIDEON. Mississippi.
HELENA. I was also raised in the South.
GIDEON. No kidding, you're a Southern girl?
HELENA. Arlington, Virginia ...
GIDEON. Well, Helena, the South welcomes you back home. Welcome home. *(Helena kisses him on the lips.)* Me and my wife should have you over for dinner some night. *(Pause.)*
HELENA. Wow, you're married. That is great, that is so great. When did you get married?
GIDEON. Going on twelve years now.
HELENA. High-school sweethearts?
GIDEON. Met in a bar.
HELENA. Any kids?
GIDEON. Six. *(Beat.)*
HELENA. Six? You have six kids?
GIDEON. Ben, Megan, Rachel, Christian, Nick, and little Bethy.
HELENA. There's really no common ground here. Wow. Can I ask you something?

GIDEON. Shoot.
HELENA. How old are you?
GIDEON. I'm thirty-four.
HELENA. I'm thirty-four.
GIDEON. Something in common, then.

Scene 17

Linda's house, Ireland

Lunchtime.

LINDA. Anna is just lovely.
ADAM. Oh, I like Sean *very* much. Great guy.
LINDA. Good kids.
ADAM. Yes they are.
LINDA. I need to talk to you about the wedding. Before they get back. To get to those cliffs, you have to walk.
ADAM. Anna said it's quite a way.
LINDA. Twenty minutes across the heather.
ADAM. Anna said you're a little agoraphobic.
LINDA. That's right.
ADAM. I was surprised when they told me where they were getting married. Seems a little selfish of them.
LINDA. No, they asked me. When they came back to tell me they were getting married, Sean said, "Mammy, we'd like to do it on the cliffs." And what could I say? I said, "I think that's perfect."
ADAM. Are you concerned you won't be able to ... should we push for a change of venue, do you think? After all the weather is against us anyway.
LINDA. No. I will walk on my two legs to those cliffs and I will stand there and watch my son marry. I promise you that. I wanted to tell you I was afraid. I might need your arm. I might need a man on steady legs beside me, understanding. My brother will be there but so will his wife. He'll be taken up with her, she'll probably be complaining about getting her heels stuck in the mud or something.

ADAM. I'd be happy to.

LINDA. Maybe take my arm or something.

ADAM. No problem.

LINDA. Thank you. Sean said you've traveled all over the world, seen all kinds of things, fought all kinds of battles you're not even allowed to talk about. He looks up to you. *(Beat.)* I expect you're almost never afraid.

ADAM. I was afraid ten minutes ago. I was afraid to ring your doorbell. A strange country, a strange house.

LINDA. It's kind of you to tell me that.

ADAM. I was afraid to get on the airplane. Afraid to come. All by myself. No wife. No ... no other person. I will be grateful for your arm on the day of the wedding.

LINDA. I used to go to the cliffs all the time when I was a girl. Sean's right. It is the most beautiful view in all the world. *(Beat.)* I was raped there when Sean was eight years old. That was the last time I went.

ADAM. Do the kids understand what they're asking you to do?

LINDA. Not at all. They know that it happened. They don't know where. I would never tell them. This man, he took away many things from me, he never knew, I think, he was taking. There was a child. I aborted the child. The church aborted me. My husband left. My son and daughter grew up with a useless mother and no father at all. But I would not let this man destroy Sean's favorite place in all the world. And now I'm going back to watch my son marry there. And perhaps now *I* win.

Scene 18

Linda's house, Donegal

Linda, Adam, Max, and Helena all talking loudly, on top of each other, as big families do. That's the important thing. A cacophony.

MAX. It's going to rain —
HELENA. But Anna says —
LINDA. Sean is dead set on —
MAX. The forecast says rain, my darlings.
LINDA. What does it matter if people get wet? It's a tiny wedding.
HELENA. These are friends! They won't care if —
ADAM. But you have to consider, people have flown in —
HELENA. Is there a way we can erect a tent?
MAX. Not by tomorrow morning.
LINDA. The weather forecast isn't always right, you know. In fact it's always wrong! *(Blackout. The sound of bells, not wedding bells, but a clock striking the time. Then, a howling wind.)*

Scene 19

The cliffs of Donegal

We see the people we know — Adam, Linda, and Max, standing in raincoats. The rest of the cast is onstage, as wedding guests.

Helena fights to make herself heard above the wind and rain.

HELENA. Hello, I'm Helena and I will be officiating today. This is the first time I have done this, so as you can imagine, I am both excited and a little nervous — much as I imagine Anna and Sean are. It is, after all, the first time that they have done this too. I am not here as a representative of any church, or of any state. I have not been arbitrarily ordained on the internet. I am here not to marry them, but to witness with all of you as they choose to marry each other. And what we are witnessing is the birth of a new family. *(The wedding scene remains, at least at first, but what we hear and probably see is Anna and Sean late at night, their first real conversation.)*
SEAN. Tell me about where you grew up. The place you were born.
ANNA. Countryside.
SEAN. Yeah?
ANNA. Tall grass. Watercolor colors. That kind of thing. A lot of space. A lot of sunshine. A lot of play. I was a happy child. I didn't see my father much —
SEAN. How come?
ANNA. He's in the military.
SEAN. Army? *(Anna nods.)*
ANNA. When I did it was a treat, and when he was gone I had my mother all to myself. That's what every child wants anyway. I was lucky. Very, very lucky, I think. Of course that's what made it so hard when she died. That she was my best friend. My therapist says —
SEAN. You have a therapist?

ANNA. Uh-huh. *(Pause.)* This is New York City, that's what we do.

SEAN. Sure.

ANNA. Wow.

SEAN. What?

ANNA. You're making me feel really uncomfortable.

SEAN. Why?

ANNA. Because I say I have a therapist and a fucking cloud covers your face like —

SEAN. No.

ANNA. Yes.

SEAN. I've dated a lot of crazies.

ANNA. Were they in therapy?

SEAN. No.

ANNA. There you go. *(Pause.)*

SEAN. I'm sorry. I interrupted. What does your therapist say? About your mother?

ANNA. Never mind.

SEAN. I'm sorry.

ANNA. She said that my mother died before I had a chance to rebel against her. So it made her death particularly ...

SEAN. Sure. *(Beat.)* My father died of a heart attack when I was eighteen.

ANNA. I'm sorry.

SEAN. I hadn't seen him for years. He left my mother. I think I stopped loving him. When he died, I felt sad. But relieved almost. Free.

ANNA. I don't like the word "crazies." I like the word "troubled." You've dated a lot of *troubled* women.

SEAN. Have I?

ANNA. Apparently. *(Beat.)* I'm not troubled anymore. Fragile sometimes, but I'm not troubled.

SEAN. That's nice.

ANNA. Tell me about where *you* grew up.

SEAN. Town. Covered in mist usually. Small town. Stony. Grey. Near the sea.

ANNA. Happy?

SEAN. No. Not me. I wasn't. Sometimes I was. But mostly sad. My mother was very sad, you see. Something bad happened to her and she never got over it. So when I was growing up, the sadness was like the mist, you know. Fucking everywhere.

ANNA. It's awful, isn't it?
SEAN. What is?
ANNA. Getting to know someone.

Scene 20

Two figures, briefly illuminated

*Anna and Sean are the only people onstage. They are some-
where quiet.*

SEAN. A few drops of rain never hurt anybody.
ANNA. Could you even hear what you were agreeing to?
SEAN. I could hear. Could you?
ANNA. Yes.
SEAN. It was perfect.
ANNA. It was perfect. *(Pause.)*
SEAN. I wish we didn't have to die.
ANNA. We won't. Not for a long time yet. Not for a long time.

End of Play

PROPERTY LIST

Dead dog
Cell phones
Flashlight
Small gardening tool
Phones
Sandwiches
Bag with thick manuscript
Drinks
Cell phone
Abstract modern sculpture
Treadmill
Notebook
Books
Bag with food
Bag with large book
Rifle

SOUND EFFECTS

Party sounds
Microphone screech
Machine beeping
Answering machine message
Phone rings
Bear growling
Gunshot
Bells
Clock striking the time
Howling wind
Wind and rain

NEW PLAYS

★ **YELLOW FACE by David Henry Hwang.** Asian-American playwright DHH leads a protest against the casting of Jonathan Pryce as the Eurasian pimp in the original Broadway production of *Miss Saigon*, condemning the practice as "yellowface." The lines between truth and fiction blur with hilarious and moving results in this unreliable memoir. "A pungent play of ideas with a big heart." *—Variety.* "Fabulously inventive." *—The New Yorker.* [5M, 2W] ISBN: 978-0-8222-2301-6

★ **33 VARIATIONS by Moisés Kaufmann.** A mother coming to terms with her daughter. A composer coming to terms with his genius. And, even though they're separated by 200 years, these two people share an obsession that might, even just for a moment, make time stand still. "A compellingly original and thoroughly watchable play for today." *—Talkin' Broadway.* [4M, 4W] ISBN: 978-0-8222-2392-4

★ **BOOM by Peter Sinn Nachtrieb.** A grad student's online personal ad lures a mysterious journalism student to his subterranean research lab. But when a major catastrophic event strikes the planet, their date takes on evolutionary significance and the fate of humanity hangs in the balance. "Darkly funny dialogue." *—NY Times.* "Literate, coarse, thoughtful, sweet, scabrously inappropriate." *—Washington City Paper.* [1M, 2W] ISBN: 978-0-8222-2370-2

★ **LOVE, LOSS AND WHAT I WORE by Nora Ephron and Delia Ephron, based on the book by Ilene Beckerman.** A play of monologues and ensemble pieces about women, clothes and memory covering all the important subjects—mothers, prom dresses, mothers, buying bras, mothers, hating purses and why we only wear black. "Funny, compelling." *—NY Times.* "So funny and so powerful." *—WowOwow.com.* [5W] ISBN: 978-0-8222-2355-9

★ **CIRCLE MIRROR TRANSFORMATION by Annie Baker.** When four lost New Englanders enrolled in Marty's community center drama class experiment with harmless games, hearts are quietly torn apart, and tiny wars of epic proportions are waged and won. "Absorbing, unblinking and sharply funny." *—NY Times.* [2M, 3W] ISBN: 978-0-8222-2445-7

★ **BROKE-OLOGY by Nathan Louis Jackson.** The King family has weathered the hardships of life and survived with their love for each other intact. But when two brothers are called home to take care of their father, they find themselves strangely at odds. "Engaging dialogue." *—TheaterMania.com.* "Assured, bighearted." *—Time Out.* [3M, 1W] ISBN: 978-0-8222-2428-0

DRAMATISTS PLAY SERVICE, INC.
440 Park Avenue South, New York, NY 10016 212-683-8960 Fax 212-213-1539
postmaster@dramatists.com   www.dramatists.com

NEW PLAYS

★ **A CIVIL WAR CHRISTMAS: AN AMERICAN MUSICAL CELEBRA-TION by Paula Vogel, music by Daryl Waters.** It's 1864, and Washington, D.C. is settling down to the coldest Christmas Eve in years. Intertwining many lives, this musical shows us that the gladness of one's heart is the best gift of all. "Boldly inventive theater, warm and affecting." –*Talkin' Broadway.* "Crisp strokes of dialogue." –*NY Times.* [12M, 5W] ISBN: 978-0-8222-2361-0

★ **SPEECH & DEBATE by Stephen Karam.** Three teenage misfits in Salem, Oregon discover they are linked by a sex scandal that's rocked their town. "Savvy comedy." –*Variety.* "Hilarious, cliché-free, and immensely entertaining." –*NY Times.* "A strong, rangy play." –*NY Newsday.* [2M, 2W] ISBN: 978-0-8222-2286-6

★ **DIVIDING THE ESTATE by Horton Foote.** Matriarch Stella Gordon is determined not to divide her 100-year-old Texas estate, despite her family's declining wealth and the looming financial crisis. But her three children have another plan. "Goes for laughs and succeeds." –*NY Daily News.* "The theatrical equivalent of a page-turner." –*Bloomberg.com.* [4M, 9W] ISBN: 978-0-8222-2398-6

★ **WHY TORTURE IS WRONG, AND THE PEOPLE WHO LOVE THEM by Christopher Durang.** Christopher Durang turns political humor upside down with this raucous and provocative satire about America's growing homeland "insecurity." "A smashing new play." –*NY Observer.* "You may laugh yourself silly." –*Bloomberg News.* [4M, 3W] ISBN: 978-0-8222-2401-3

★ **FIFTY WORDS by Michael Weller.** While their nine-year-old son is away for the night on his first sleepover, Adam and Jan have an evening alone together, beginning a suspenseful nightlong roller-coaster ride of revelation, rancor, passion and humor. "Mr. Weller is a bold and productive dramatist." –*NY Times.* [1M, 1W] ISBN: 978-0-8222-2348-1

★ **BECKY'S NEW CAR by Steven Dietz.** Becky Foster is caught in middle age, middle management and in a middling marriage—with no prospects for change on the horizon. Then one night a socially inept and grief-struck millionaire stumbles into the car dealership where Becky works. "Gently and consistently funny." –*Variety.* "Perfect blend of hilarious comedy and substantial weight." –*Broadway Hour.* [4M, 3W] ISBN: 978-0-8222-2393-1

DRAMATISTS PLAY SERVICE, INC.
440 Park Avenue South, New York, NY 10016 212-683-8960 Fax 212-213-1539
postmaster@dramatists.com www.dramatists.com

NEW PLAYS

★ **AT HOME AT THE ZOO by Edward Albee.** Edward Albee delves deeper into his play THE ZOO STORY by adding a first act, HOMELIFE, which precedes Peter's fateful meeting with Jerry on a park bench in Central Park. "An essential and heartening experience." *—NY Times.* "Darkly comic and thrilling." *—Time Out.* "Genuinely fascinating." *—Journal News.* [2M, 1W] ISBN: 978-0-8222-2317-7

★ **PASSING STRANGE book and lyrics by Stew, music by Stew and Heidi Rodewald, created in collaboration with Annie Dorsen.** A daring musical about a young bohemian that takes you from black middle-class America to Amsterdam, Berlin and beyond on a journey towards personal and artistic authenticity. "Fresh, exuberant, bracingly inventive, bitingly funny, and full of heart." *—NY Times.* "The freshest musical in town!" *—Wall Street Journal.* "Excellent songs and a vulnerable heart." *—Variety.* [4M, 3W] ISBN: 978-0-8222-2400-6

★ **REASONS TO BE PRETTY by Neil LaBute.** Greg really, truly adores his girlfriend, Steph. Unfortunately, he also thinks she has a few physical imperfections, and when he mentions them, all hell breaks loose. "Tight, tense and emotionally true." *—Time Magazine.* "Lively and compulsively watchable." *—The Record.* [2M, 2W] ISBN: 978-0-8222-2394-8

★ **OPUS by Michael Hollinger.** With only a few days to rehearse a grueling Beethoven masterpiece, a world-class string quartet struggles to prepare their highest-profile performance ever—a televised ceremony at the White House. "Intimate, intense and profoundly moving." *—Time Out.* "Worthy of scores of bravissimos." *—BroadwayWorld.com.* [4M, 1W] ISBN: 978-0-8222-2363-4

★ **BECKY SHAW by Gina Gionfriddo.** When an evening calculated to bring happiness takes a dark turn, crisis and comedy ensue in this wickedly funny play that asks what we owe the people we love and the strangers who land on our doorstep. "As engrossing as it is ferociously funny." *—NY Times.* "Gionfriddo is some kind of genius." *—Variety.* [2M, 3W] ISBN: 978-0-8222-2402-0

★ **KICKING A DEAD HORSE by Sam Shepard.** Hobart Struther's horse has just dropped dead. In an eighty-minute monologue, he discusses what path brought him here in the first place, the fate of his marriage, his career, politics and eventually the nature of the universe. "Deeply instinctual and intuitive." *—NY Times.* "The brilliance is in the infinite reverberations Shepard extracts from his simple metaphor." *—TheaterMania.* [1M, 1W] ISBN: 978-0-8222-2336-8

DRAMATISTS PLAY SERVICE, INC.
440 Park Avenue South, New York, NY 10016 212-683-8960 Fax 212-213-1539
postmaster@dramatists.com www.dramatists.com

NEW PLAYS

★ **AUGUST: OSAGE COUNTY by Tracy Letts.** WINNER OF THE 2008 PULITZER PRIZE AND TONY AWARD. When the large Weston family reunites after Dad disappears, their Oklahoma homestead explodes in a maelstrom of repressed truths and unsettling secrets. "Fiercely funny and bitingly sad." *–NY Times.* "Ferociously entertaining." *–Variety.* "A hugely ambitious, highly combustible saga." *–NY Daily News.* [6M, 7W] ISBN: 978-0-8222-2300-9

★ **RUINED by Lynn Nottage.** WINNER OF THE 2009 PULITZER PRIZE. Set in a small mining town in Democratic Republic of Congo, RUINED is a haunting, probing work about the resilience of the human spirit during times of war. "A full-immersion drama of shocking complexity and moral ambiguity." *–Variety.* "Sincere, passionate, courageous." *–Chicago Tribune.* [8M, 4W] ISBN: 978-0-8222-2390-0

★ **GOD OF CARNAGE by Yasmina Reza, translated by Christopher Hampton.** WINNER OF THE 2009 TONY AWARD. A playground altercation between boys brings together their Brooklyn parents, leaving the couples in tatters as the rum flows and tensions explode. "Satisfyingly primitive entertainment." *–NY Times.* "Elegant, acerbic, entertainingly fueled on pure bile." *–Variety.* [2M, 2W] ISBN: 978-0-8222-2399-3

★ **THE SEAFARER by Conor McPherson.** Sharky has returned to Dublin to look after his irascible, aging brother. Old drinking buddies Ivan and Nicky are holed up at the house too, hoping to play some cards. But with the arrival of a stranger from the distant past, the stakes are raised ever higher. "Dark and enthralling Christmas fable." *–NY Times.* "A timeless classic." *–Hollywood Reporter.* [5M] ISBN: 978-0-8222-2284-2

★ **THE NEW CENTURY by Paul Rudnick.** When the playwright is Paul Rudnick, expectations are geared for a play both hilarious and smart, and this provocative and outrageous comedy is no exception. "The one-liners fly like rockets." *–NY Times.* "The funniest playwright around." *–Journal News.* [2M, 3W] ISBN: 978-0-8222-2315-3

★ **SHIPWRECKED! AN ENTERTAINMENT—THE AMAZING ADVENTURES OF LOUIS DE ROUGEMONT (AS TOLD BY HIMSELF) by Donald Margulies.** The amazing story of bravery, survival and celebrity that left nineteenth-century England spellbound. Dare to be whisked away. "A deft, literate narrative." *–LA Times.* "Springs to life like a theatrical pop-up book." *–NY Times.* [2M, 1W] ISBN: 978-0-8222-2341-2

DRAMATISTS PLAY SERVICE, INC.
440 Park Avenue South, New York, NY 10016 212-683-8960 Fax 212-213-1539
postmaster@dramatists.com www.dramatists.com